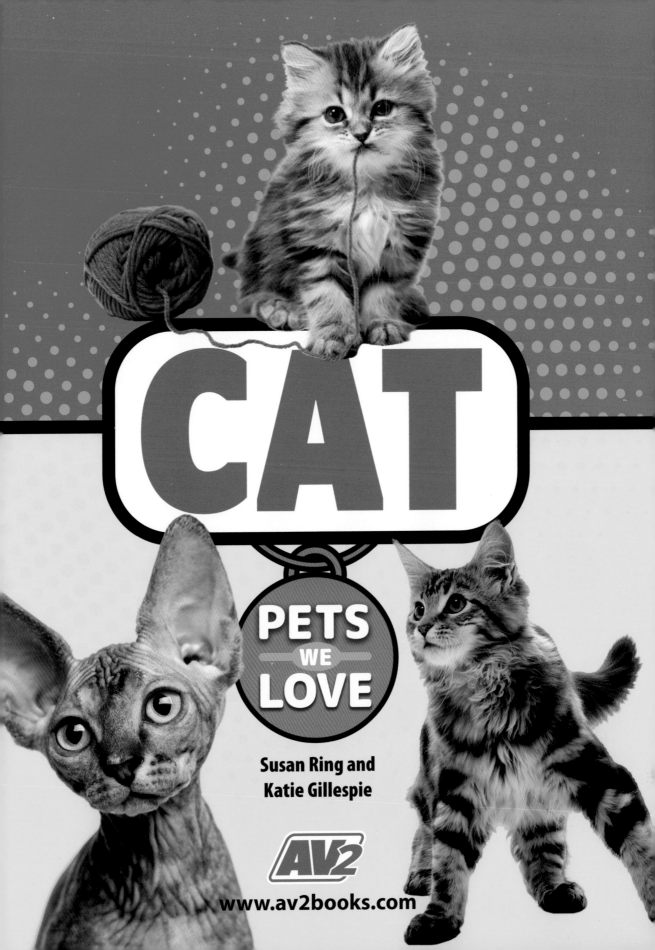

CAT

PETS WE LOVE

Susan Ring and
Katie Gillespie

AV2

www.av2books.com

Step 1
Go to **www.av2books.com**

Step 2
Enter this unique code

ICRTKBC32

Step 3
Explore your interactive eBook!

CONTENTS

4   Cat Care
6   From Wild to Mild
8   Pet Profile
10   Picking Your Pet
12   Life Cycle
14   Cat Supplies
16   Feeding a Feline
18   Fast and Furry
20   Purr-fect Grooming
22   Healthy and Happy
24   Cat Behavior
26   Cat Tales
28   Pet Puzzlers
30   Calling Your Cat
31   Key Words

AV2 is optimized for use on any device

Your interactive eBook comes with...

Contents
Browse a live contents page to easily navigate through resources

Audio
Listen to sections of the book read aloud

Videos
Watch informative video clips

Weblinks
Gain additional information for research

Try This!
Complete activities and hands-on experiments

Key Words
Study vocabulary, and complete a matching word activity

Quizzes
Test your knowledge

Slideshows
View images and captions

... and much, much more!

PETS WE LOVE CAT

Contents

2 AV2 Book Code

4 Cat Care

6 From Wild to Mild

8 Pet Profile

10 Picking Your Pet

12 Life Cycle

14 Cat Supplies

16 Feeding a Feline

18 Fast and Furry

20 Purr-fect Grooming

22 Healthy and Happy

24 Cat Behavior

26 Cat Tales

28 Pet Puzzlers

30 Calling Your Cat

31 Key Words/Index

Cat Care

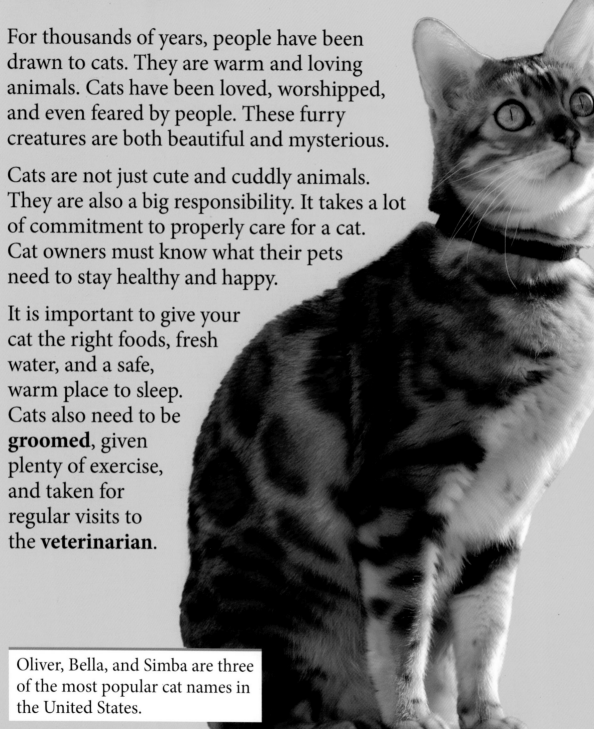

For thousands of years, people have been drawn to cats. They are warm and loving animals. Cats have been loved, worshipped, and even feared by people. These furry creatures are both beautiful and mysterious.

Cats are not just cute and cuddly animals. They are also a big responsibility. It takes a lot of commitment to properly care for a cat. Cat owners must know what their pets need to stay healthy and happy.

It is important to give your cat the right foods, fresh water, and a safe, warm place to sleep. Cats also need to be **groomed**, given plenty of exercise, and taken for regular visits to the **veterinarian**.

Oliver, Bella, and Simba are three of the most popular cat names in the United States.

There are about
75 million
pet cats in the
United States.

About **30** percent
of households in the
United States own
a cat.

Some cats are born with
**six or more
toes** on each paw.

There are more than **600 million** domestic cats on Earth.

Ancient **saber-toothed cats** had teeth up to **8 inches** long. (20 centimeters)

Millions of cats were **mummified** in ancient Egypt.

As pets, **African wildcats** can live up to **15 years**.

Ancient Egyptians worshipped cats.

From Wild to Mild

Cats have been around for millions of years. This has been proven by the discovery of ancient **fossils**. These fossils belong to a creature called *Miacis*. This weasel-like animal lived about 50 million years ago.

Scientists think that cats and humans have lived together for as long as 5,000 years. In ancient Egypt, cats and people had such a close relationship that they were buried together when they died.

The most likely relatives of modern house cats are African wildcats. They were domesticated by the ancient Egyptians in 2,500 BC. These wildcats were very useful to the Egyptians because they ate mice. This helped protect people's crops from the pesky rodents, who liked eating grain.

The Egyptians enjoyed having the wildcats around. They fed and cared for the friendliest cats. Over time, the wildcats became like pets to the Egyptians.

Domestic cats are related to lions, tigers, and leopards.

Pet Profile

There are many different **breeds** of cats. They come in a variety of colors, shapes, and sizes. Most house cats are **mixed-breed** cats. Other cats are purebred. This means that the same features have been passed on from generation to generation. Each breed of cat has distinct traits that make it special. Manx cats do not have a tail. Turkish Van cats have waterproof fur.

Domestic Cats
- Include all **unpedigreed** cats
- Are one of the most common house cats
- Can be long-haired or short-haired
- Come in several sizes and shapes
- Have a variety of colors and markings
- Can have many different temperaments

Sphynxes
- Have wrinkly skin
- Do not have any whiskers or hair
- Enjoy being watched
- Do not like to be the only pet in the household
- Originated in 1966
- The first Sphynx came from furry parents

Ragdolls

- Have light-colored body fur
- Have darker fur around their legs, tail, face, and ears
- Are friendly with children
- Have a very laid-back personality
- Enjoy grooming
- Have a long and silky coat
- Need to be brushed and combed often

Persians

- Are a very loving breed
- Have long and fluffy fur
- Need plenty of daily combing, brushing, and grooming
- Come in many colors
- Have a stocky body
- Are generally quiet
- Have a flat face

Siamese

- Are an intelligent breed of cat
- Have a tan body with a dark tail, ears, paws, and head
- Can be very independent
- Have large and pointed ears
- Are quite vocal and meow loudly

Scottish Folds

- Are easily adaptable to changes in their environment
- Are born with straight ears
- At 3 weeks of age, their ears fold forward
- Can be many different colors
- Have a sweet and loving temperament
- Can have long or short hair

Up to **95 percent** of pet owners consider their pets to be **family members**.

Domestic cats live about **15 years** on average.

A **20-year-old** house cat is as aged as a **96-year-old** human.

It is important to consider how your cat will get along with other pets in your home.

Picking Your Pet

Before choosing your pet cat, there are many important factors to consider. Research different breeds to find one that will be the best fit for your family. Think about these questions before choosing your furry friend.

How Much Will a Cat Cost?

The price of your pet cat will vary depending on where you go. Many cities have animal shelters, where pets have been rescued from the streets. Shelter cats are just waiting for a good home. The most expensive cats are purebreds. Make sure to consider other costs, such as food, bedding, litter, and toys, for your pet cat.

How Much Time Will My Cat Need?

Kittens can be very frisky and active. They need plenty of attention. Adult cats may require less time to care for than a kitten. Keep in mind your pet's grooming needs as well. A long-haired cat must be brushed and groomed every day. Short-haired cats can be groomed less often. All cats need their litter boxes cleaned every day.

How Will a Cat Affect My Family?

You must be careful when bringing home a new cat. It is important to make sure that no one in your family has allergies. Exposing an allergic parent or sibling to a pet can be very dangerous.

Life Cycle

Your cat's needs will change as she gets older. It is fun to play with a small, cute kitten. It is just as important to make time for an adult cat. Your pet will depend on you throughout her lifetime.

Newborn Kitten

Kittens are born completely helpless. Their eyes are closed and will not open for 8 to 12 days. They cannot walk very well. Instead, kittens crawl. Most of their time is spent sleeping and drinking their mothers' milk. Always wash your hands before handling a newborn kitten. Germs on your hands can make a newborn kitten sick.

More than 10 Years

As they get older, cats begin to need more sleep. They are less active. Their hearing and eyesight may begin to fail. Senior cats may still be playful. They may require a special diet, as some foods are hard to digest. Extra nutrients may also be needed.

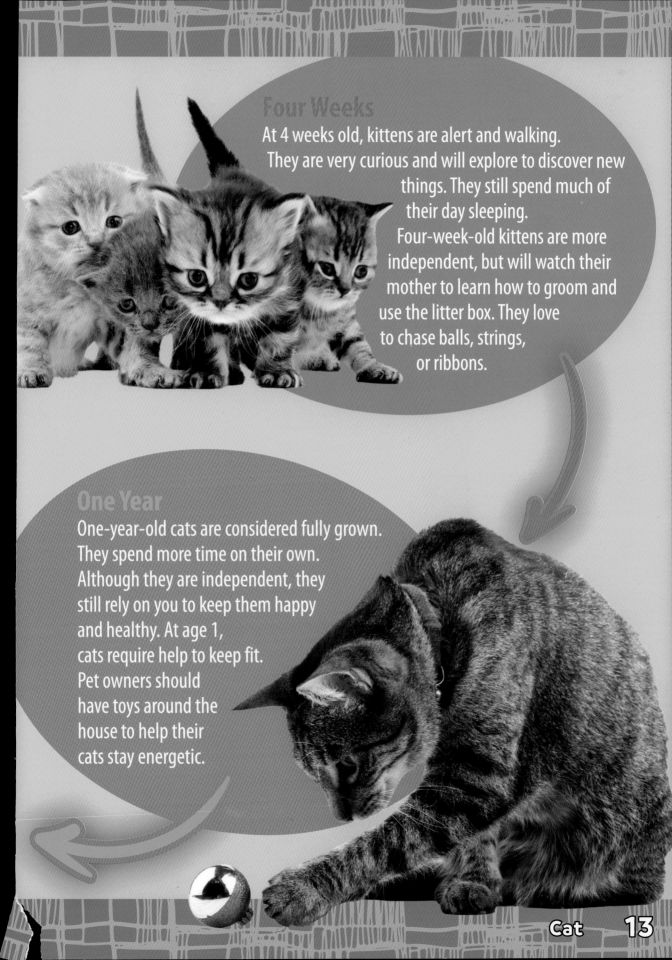

Four Weeks

At 4 weeks old, kittens are alert and walking. They are very curious and will explore to discover new things. They still spend much of their day sleeping.

Four-week-old kittens are more independent, but will watch their mother to learn how to groom and use the litter box. They love to chase balls, strings, or ribbons.

One Year

One-year-old cats are considered fully grown. They spend more time on their own. Although they are independent, they still rely on you to keep them happy and healthy. At age 1, cats require help to keep fit. Pet owners should have toys around the house to help their cats stay energetic.

Cats sleep for an average
of 15 hours a day.

Cat Supplies

There are some basic supplies you will need before you bring home your new pet. These include a litter box, a comfortable bed, and dishes for food and water.

Your cat should have toys to help stay active and alert. A scratching post can also be useful. This will protect your furniture, but still allow your cat to sharpen his claws. Very young kittens may need a hot-water bottle or a ticking clock in their bed. These can help them to feel less lonely.

Cleanliness is very important to cats. You must have a quality brush or a comb to keep your pet cat's fur groomed. The kind of brush may depend on the length and type of your cat's hair.

Both indoor and outdoor cats require a litter box. It should never be kept near the cat's bed, food dish, or water dish. The litter box can be covered or open. Some cats may be trained to use a toilet. They do not need a litter box at all.

A cat's bed can be bought from a pet supply store. It should be warm and placed away from drafts. Some cats are just as happy sleeping in a blanket-lined cardboard box as in a bed. Do not be surprised if your cat chooses his own sleeping arrangements. Many cats enjoy having a special spot that is their own.

Cats have small "hooks" on their tongues. These are useful for tearing up food.

Feeding a Feline

Cats can be quite fussy when it comes to meals. This is why you must change your cat's food from time to time. If you do not vary what your cat eats, she may become so used to one food that she refuses to eat anything else.

What Should I Feed My Cat?

Cat food comes in different formulas. Canned wet food is available in a variety of flavors. It can give your cat all of the vitamins she needs to stay healthy. You should also feed your cat dry food. It helps to clean and strengthen your cat's teeth. Most pet owners give their cats a balance of half wet and half dry food. On occasion, you may also want to feed your cat fresh food. Cats love to eat turkey or chicken. When feeding your cat fresh fish, it is important to remove all of the bones. You must also make sure to keep your cat's water dish full. Change the water often to keep it fresh and clean.

What Do Cats Like?

Most cats love treats. These come in many different sizes, shapes, and flavors. Make sure you only give your cat treats once in a while. They do not offer as much nutrition as your cat's food. It is also important for cats to have some fat in their diet. Their bodies are unable to produce it on their own.

Fast and Furry

From domestic cats to wildcats, all cats have certain features in common. The majority of cats have fur on their bodies. This helps to keep them warm.

Cats are quick, strong, **agile**, and intelligent. They have keen senses, which are very sensitive. These traits make cats exceptionally good hunters.

Nose

Cats have a very sharp sense of smell. Kittens use it to guide them before they are able to see.

Eyes

In low light, a cat's pupils grow very round and large. In bright light, a cat's pupils narrow to slits.

Ears

A cat's ears can move independently. They turn up to 180 degrees to locate sounds.

Mouth

Cats have rough tongues for drinking and grooming. They use their sharp, pointed teeth to rip meat.

Paws

A cat's paws are protected by tough pads. The paws also have sharp, **retractable** claws.

Whiskers

Cats use their whiskers to judge whether their bodies will fit in tight spaces.

Legs

Cats have very strong back legs. They walk by moving both their left legs, then both their right legs. This lets cats walk quickly and silently.

Tail

A cat's tail is an extension of its backbone. Cats use it for balance and to show their moods.

Most cats do not need to be bathed. Instead, they lick their coats to keep themselves clean.

Purr-fect Grooming

It is normal for your cat to spend a lot of time grooming himself. Cats use their rough tongues like combs to remove dirt and twigs from their fur. They also lick their paws and use them to clean their faces, like a washcloth.

Cats need to be groomed by their owners as well. Regular grooming can help a kitten adapt to being handled. It also allows you to check your cat's skin and fur for burrs or **mats**.

It is important to brush your cat often, especially if he has long hair. This will prevent knots and tangles. To groom your cat, hold him on your lap or in front of you on the floor.

Slowly check your cat's whole body for anything out of the ordinary. Then, brush downward gently. You should move from the head to the tail. After brushing, you should use a comb to finish grooming a long-haired cat.

Your cat may purr when he is being brushed. Regular grooming helps prevent hair balls. If a cat swallows too much fur while grooming himself, this fur can block the stomach. Keeping your cat groomed will make sure he is healthy. It will also create a bond between you and your cat.

Cats should visit the vet once or twice a year.

Kittens should get their first **vaccines** when they are about 8 weeks old.

A cat's normal **heart rate** is 140 to 220 beats per minute.

A cat's average **temperature** is 100° to 103° Fahrenheit. (38° to 39° Celsius)

Healthy and Happy

A healthy cat is a happy cat. Loving and caring for your cat will help keep her happy. You should also make sure your cat is well groomed, given the right foods, and getting regular exercise. Take your pet to a veterinarian who makes you and your cat feel comfortable.

Your veterinarian will be able to answer any questions you may have about your cat's health or behavior. He will also give your cat regular **vaccinations**. These will protect your cat from common illnesses.

Different types of cats have special concerns. Light-colored cats are easily sunburned. It is best for them to stay out of the sunlight, when possible.

You will get to know your cat's personality over time. As you do, you will learn her habits and patterns. This will help you to notice if something is wrong. Pay attention to your cat's schedule. Is she eating more or less than normal? Is she drinking more water than usual? If so, this could mean that your cat is sick.

Sneezing or coughing are other symptoms that may mean your cat is sick. Be aware of any wound licking or limping. These might indicate that your cat needs veterinary care. It is important for you to make sure that your home is safe for your cat.

Cats make different sounds when they are scared, angry, or happy. Over time, you will learn to understand how your cat feels when he hisses or purrs.

Cat Behavior

Although cats are often independent, they do like to play and bond with their owner. Indoor cats require plenty of toys and activities. Outdoor cats need attention, too. It is important for you to love and spend time with your cat.

Cats are very intelligent. They can be trained and disciplined. If your cat behaves badly, correct him with a firm "no." Never hit your cat if he is naughty. When your cat does something nice, reward him with a hug or a treat.

Your cat will communicate with you in many ways. Even though he cannot speak, he can let you know how he is feeling. Your cat may move his tail to show that he is upset or excited. When he is grooming, your cat probably wants to be left alone. When he rubs his head against you, he wants attention.

Cats have special scent glands between their eye and ear. Rubbing them against objects or people will mark them. Your cat will feel more comfortable when he recognizes his own scent on you.

Tweety and Sylvester
cartoons have won
two Academy Awards.

From authors to inventors, many important people have been friends of felines. Mark Twain, who wrote *The Adventures of Huckleberry Finn*; Daniel Boone, the legendary American frontiersman; and Sir Isaac Newton, who discovered the theory of gravity and invented the first cat-flap door, are all well known for their fondness for cats.

Several U.S. presidents have also been identified as cat lovers, including Abraham Lincoln. President Theodore Roosevelt owned a gray cat named Slippers, who had six toes on each foot. Slippers was allowed to attend large state dinners at the White House and sit wherever he wanted. Before he became president, Governor Ronald Reagan signed a bill that made it illegal to kick cats.

Cats have also been featured in a variety of television shows, movies, books, fables, and stories. Sylvester the Cat is best recognized for appearing with Tweety Bird in more than 40 cartoons.

Of Cats and Men

People often develop meaningful relationships with their pets. Approximately 95 percent of cat owners admit that they talk to their furry friends on a regular basis. Cats can be an important part of their owners' lives. They are typically thought of as members of the family.

Pet Puzzlers

What do you know about cats? If you can answer the following questions correctly, you may be ready to own a cat.

1 What culture worshipped cats?

2 Which breed of cat is quite vocal and meows loudly?

3 Why must you wash your hands when handling a newborn kitten?

4 What are some supplies you need for your pet cat?

5 What should you feed your cat?

6 What do cats use their whiskers for?

7 Why is regular grooming so important?

8 When should your kitten first be vaccinated?

9 How should you reward your cat?

10 How do cats communicate with their owners?

ANSWERS

1. Ancient Egypt   2. Siamese   3. Newborn kittens are very sensitive, and germs on your hands might make them sick.   4. A warm bed, toys, food and water dishes, a brush and comb, and a litter box   5. A combination of wet food, dry food, fresh food, and treats   6. To judge whether their bodies will fit in tight spaces   7. Regular grooming helps to keep your cat healthy. It prevents hair balls from forming and allows you to form a bond with your cat.   8. Around 8 weeks of age   9. With a hug or a treat   10. By moving their tails, making purring or hissing noises, and rubbing their heads on their owners

Calling Your Cat

Before you bring home your pet cat, brainstorm some cat names you like. Some names may work better for a female cat. Others may suit a male cat. Here are just a few suggestions.

Kitty

Garfield

Sylvester

Ginger

Fluffy

Snuggles

Smokey

Socks

Sam

Key Words

agile: athletic; moves easily

breeds: groups of animals that share specific characteristics

fossils: remains of animals and plants from long ago, found in rocks

groomed: cleaned by removing dirt from fur

mats: tangles, knots, and clumps of fur

mixed-breed: a cat whose parents and relatives are a mixture of different cat breeds

retractable: able to withdraw

unpedigreed: not having a pure line of ancestors

vaccinations: injections of medicines that help prevent certain diseases or illnesses

veterinarian: animal doctor

Index

African wildcats 6, 7

behavior 23

breeds 8, 9, 11

claws 15, 19

domestic cats 5, 7, 8, 10, 18

food 4, 11, 12, 15, 16, 17, 23

grooming 4, 9, 11, 13, 15, 18, 21, 23, 25

health 23

life cycle 12

Persians 9

ragdolls 9

Siamese 9, 29

Sphynxes 8

supplies 15, 28

veterinarian 4, 22, 23

Get the best of both worlds.

AV2 bridges the gap between print and digital.

The expandable resources toolbar enables quick access to content including **videos**, **audio**, **activities**, **weblinks**, **slideshows**, **quizzes**, and **key words**.

Animated videos make static images come alive.

Resource icons on each page help readers to further **explore key concepts**.

Published by AV2
350 5th Avenue, 59th Floor
New York, NY 10118
Website: www.av2books.com

Library of Congress Cataloging-in-Publication Data

Names: Ring, Susan, author. | Gillespie, Katie, author.
Title: Cat / Susan Ring and Katie Gillespie.
Description: New York, NY : AV2 by Weigl, [2020] | Series: Pets we love |
Includes index. | Audience: Grades 4-6 |
Identifiers: LCCN 2019048002 (print) | LCCN 2019048003 (ebook) | ISBN
9781791119126 (library binding) | ISBN 9781791119133 (paperback) | ISBN
 9781791119140 (ebook other) | ISBN 9781791119157 (ebook other)
Subjects: LCSH: Cats--Juvenile literature.
Classification: LCC SF447 .R563 2020 (print) | LCC SF447 (ebook) |
DDC 636.8--dc23

LC record available at https://lccn.loc.gov/2019048002
LC ebook record available at https://lccn.loc.gov/2019048003

Printed in Guangzhou, China
1 2 3 4 5 6 7 8 9 0 24 23 22 21 20

022020
101319

Project Coordinator Sara Cucini
Art Director Terry Paulhus

Photo Credits
Every reasonable effort has been made to trace ownership and to obtain permission to reprint copyright material. The publishers would be pleased to have any errors or omissions brought to their attention so that they may be corrected in subsequent printings. AV2 acknowledges Getty Images, Alamy, and Shutterstock as its primary photo suppliers for this title.